CW01590238

turner's thoughtology

THE EXECUTIVE BRIEFCASE SERIES

VOLUME I

Y Not

entrepreneurial thinking

DRIVING PASSION WITH INTEGRITY

21st Century Books

turner's thoughtology

THE EXECUTIVE BRIEFCASE SERIES

VOLUME I

Y
Not

entrepreneurial thinking

DRIVING PASSION WITH INTEGRITY

Copyright © Colin Turner 2005

The right of Colin Turner to be identified as the Author of the Work has been asserted by him in accordance with the Copyright, Design and Patents Act 1988

Published in Great Britain in 2005 by
21st Century Books UK Ltd
30 Queen Square, Bristol, BS1 4ND

www.21stcenturybooks.uk.co.
service@21stcenturybooks.uk.com

All rights reserved. No part of this publication may be reproduced, stored in a retrieval system, or transmitted in any form or by any means, electronic, mechanical, photocopying, recording, or otherwise without the prior written permission of the publishers.

No responsibility can be accepted by the publisher for action taken as a result of information contained in this publication. Readers should take specific advice when dealing with specific situations.

Printed and bound in the UK by
The Bath Press, Lower Bristol Road,
Bath, England

British Library Cataloguing in Publication
Data available

ISBN: 1-904956-06-8

turner's thoughtology

THE EXECUTIVE BRIEFCASE SERIES

VOLUME I

Y
Not

entrepreneurial thinking

DRIVING PASSION WITH INTEGRITY

What, How and You

During thirty years in business I have learned that there is a clear common theme regardless of the perspective at which we operate – be it employee, employer, manager, director, consultant, teacher or shareholder. What is it?

Business offers the perfect example of how Man will always complicate simplicity.

When a business starts the focus of attention is on its strengths. As it becomes more successful, such attention shifts towards its competitors' strengths. In time the operation becomes more concerned with managing its weaknesses.

Moving from an internally-driven company to an externally-influenced one is neither balanced nor conducive for growth.

There are only two factors important in business.
The rest is trivia.
The first is building relationships;
the other is following through.

Why is that?

Because the only two things that all of us ever want in life are good feelings and right solutions.

Whatever business you are in, when you take the time to build relationships and follow through by providing good feelings and right solutions, then such a combination guarantees success.

Common sense perhaps, yet certainly not common practice; because the fixed-thinking within business is that it *cannot* be that simple. The conditioned tendency is that if it is too simple, then we must somehow complicate it. Why?

Doing what is 'simple' involves harder work than the easier path of complicating the issue.

For example, it is harder to write a one-page concise report than a 20 page document, though the former is easier to understand.

It is much harder for people to answer a question precisely than to be long-winded, though the former is clearer. So many feel compelled to drone on as if 'inebriated with the verbosity of their own exuberance' – as Disraeli said of his counterpart,

Gladstone, who got himself so bogged down in arguing a point that it resulted in confusing everyone – perhaps the political intent!

How many times have you personally witnessed a colleague making a meal out of answering a question; or delivering a mountain of explanation over a molehill enquiry? Were you any the wiser, or simply more frustrated? How about report reading or writing? Did you get, or make, the point respectively?

There are only 24 words in the Pythagorean Theorem, 67 in the Archimedes Principle, yet there are almost 27,000 in The EU regulations on the sale of cabbage. Who is going to read the document – the farmer?

What about simply building relationships and following through – the very life blood of a business? Or did you think that cash flow is the lifeblood? How long will any business survive without customers? Just until the money runs out, then it's back to the shareholders for more.

Why do you think shareholders are wooed more than customers? Too many must be acting simple-mindedly to invest in a complicated business, plan or idea without a customer in place. Metaphorically speaking, does it really count if the product is the best thing since sliced bread? What if everyone demands rice?

Every business irrespective of size, industry and market-place has been founded with entrepreneurial thinking. Yet inexorably it moves from being a passionately-driven one by entrepreneurially-minded *warriors* toward a process-operated one by administrative-minded *worriers*.

The majority of businesses, particularly larger organisations, are seemingly successful in spite of themselves. But does this mean they are using their full potential? No, it does not. The difficulty is that when a certain level of success is gained in brand name and product sales, a kind of professional complacency sets it.

What are the first symptoms of this complaint? Indecisiveness, or the time it takes for everyone involved to sign something off. And, later, meek acceptance of such a long-winded process with the viewpoint: who needs to be agile anyway – 'after all we are the market leaders aren't we?' An attitude, you will agree, alarmingly reminiscent of the voiced complacency at the advent of change in the silent movie industry: '*Who needs to hear actors talk anyway?*'

Though the most important competitive factor a business has is the development of its people, companies continue to struggle with the challenges to build commitment, improve communication, and above all, instil a sense of ownership; despite training initiatives and operational restructuring.

Clearly, entrepreneurial ideas have a greater certainty of being profitable and *sustaining* growth when supported by management attributes. Less accepted is that executives must develop entrepreneurial thinking – those same attributes instrumental in the founding and successful growth of their business.

What is entrepreneurial thinking? Though the term is frequently used in business few can define it simply. Most misguidedly assume it is being risk-focused, opportunist and rule breaking.

Entrepreneurial thinking is *not* about being an entrepreneur, that non-conformist individual so often assumed to be a loose canon who loses investors' good money while trying to build a business by the seat of their pants.

Such perception has derived from most entrepreneurs not applying authentic *entrepreneurial thinking* – the vital key to sustainable growth in business.

Every business is founded with entrepreneurial spirit but the required thinking essential for profitable growth is either non-existent, forgotten or has been ignored.

So, some simple definitions:

Entrepreneur is a creative innovator who acting on initiative, seeks and maximises opportunity, takes a calculated risk, and passionately drives it to a worthwhile conclusion.

'Worthwhile' because monetary or profitable objectives are not the main concern of an entrepreneur. It is the passion of what they believe in that motivates them to action. Non-profit making organisations, institutes and schools, are successful because of the entrepreneurial spirit driving them.

Entrepreneurship involves more than an individual. It involves whole teams engaged in a process of willingly working together, with mutually calculated risk to create, implement, drive and follow through an innovative idea that delivers measurable value.

Within organisations this involves an approach to management that seeks to maximise value from opportunity without constraint to existing models, structure or resources.

Entrepreneurial Thinking simplifies, adapts and adopts management and processes accordingly to gain the required agility, speed, creativity and drive in order to profitably act upon specific opportunities that are worthwhile.

In corporations 'worthwhile' means in the interests of fully realising the intended purpose of the organisation to the beneficial growth of all stakeholders involved.

Recreating entrepreneurship will revitalise any business originally founded by the very same thinking. It is not so much about reinventing as rediscovering, redefining and re-implementing such attributes that repeatedly ensure future success.

Re-instilling such thinking is the most effective way to reassure all stakeholders, re-energize people and receive the reward of success. But, bearing in mind our ability to complicate simplicity, the question remains how?

We must become aware of the way we perceive things. For our perceptions actually govern our expectations, creating prejudices.

Unwittingly we can distort what is really happening and see things that simply are not there. This makes us cynical, sceptical. Yet if our fundamental perceptions are wrong, and we are not prepared to address them, we will continue doing what we have always done; and continue getting the same results.

Both our heritage and our formative years have conditioned us to respond in a historical, rather than a functional manner. When asked why we do things in a certain way, we reply 'because of this' rather than 'to achieve this'.

A detrimental consequence is seeing the future as an extension to the past. Anything that does not fit in with our preconditioned thinking remains unseen or rejected. We become so judgemental; we forget to use our judgement.

Perhaps the most critically important time of our developmental growth is exactly that – critical. All too often we become expert in spotting what is wrong with an argument rather than what is right.

Then because we habitually strive to behave in a manner that is consistent with what we are most comfortable with, we apply the same critical eye with regard to new ideas, new innovations and creativity. Any form of 'entrepreneurial thinking' is, in our conditioned opinion, probably best avoided.

Become aware of speaking in a traditional vein and whether you are inadvertently providing barriers for improvement. Thinking that things aren't like the good old days, or hoping for a better future is not where our life is at. We must become aware of how our perceptions dramatically influence our thinking and action.

We must learn to adapt and adopt the practical principles that have been proven to work. The concepts within this executive thoughtology series will provide the valuable guidance required in a simple, uncomplicated format. But there is another factor that is essential to their successful application – it is the only variable factor involved – You.

History's most profound thinkers agreed that we become what we think about.

Solomon: *As a man thinketh in his heart, so is he.*
Buddha: *All that we are is the result of what we have thought.*
Marcus Aurelius: *A man's life is what his thoughts make of it.*
Emerson: *A man is what he thinks about all day long.*
Shakespeare: *Beware our thoughts lest they betray us.*

You become what you think about.

Being *yourself* more, rather than just *selling* yourself has a major affect on your thinking straightaway.

Christopher Morley was right: *There is only one success, to be able to spend your life in your own way.*

To be able to do so involves being passionate about what you are involved with. It involves having the integrity to follow through what is important to you.

In the east there is a wise aphorism that Man must never lose passion; for in doing so evolution is brought to a standstill. In each of our hearts we have a passion to chase which, when expressed within an ethical business arena, both individual and corporate potential is released.

Throughout my career my research, coupled with practical experience, has sought to understand the different thinking behind individuals who are confident of success, despite enduring failure, and the different motivations of the employee-minded and entrepreneurially-minded. So what makes them achieve more than their colleagues?

The foundation of personal success lies in continuous self-development; and the foundation of business success is through entrepreneurial thinking incorporating passion and integrity.

Such confident, self-assured individuals ensure both personal and business success by aligning what they do with who they are; and by driving their passion with integrity.

Y Not...*question your thinking.*
Is it founded on impediment or improvement; what you can do, or can't do?

Y Not...*question your skills at following through.*
Do you finish what you start or contact the person that you said you would?

Y Not...*question your perceptions.*
Are you aware of how you see things; do you react, or do you respond?

Y Not...*question how much you sell youself.*
Do you feel different with someone that you want something from; are you as relaxed with others as you are at home?

Non-Ownership Thinking

If the most competitive ingredient that a business has is its people, then it follows that the greatest benefit to a business is to have decisive confident people who readily take ownership for what they do.

Yet surprisingly many businesses do not retain good people. The percentage of people that leave corporations is unnecessarily high. To invest in training for the benefit of your competition may be common practice; but surely to retain such talent makes much more sense?

It is, however, a challenge to persuade employees to take ownership and to be accountable. Initiatives are implemented, structures revised, systems put in place, and training commenced, but with what result? Employees get excited; then continue to operate with Non-Ownership Thinking. There is not the transformation hoped for. Why?

Though research reveals how well people respond to high expectations, seldom does it influence the common policy of only utilising low ones.

The regularity of the refrains: 'you can't do that', 'are you allowed', 'I'll have to get back to you', I'll have to check', or 'do you have permission' is indicative of a management culture that expects employees to be just that – employee-minded.

A business culture is directly influenced by people's expectations which can be compared to doing press-ups. If you expect to do twenty, you start straining at seventeen. If you expect to do thirty, you will begin to feel the strain at twenty-seven.

In business it is always the last quarter of the financial year when everyone begins to feel the strain of meeting budget expectations. If, on the other hand, budget expectations look as if they are going to be reached in an early quarter, then everyone compensates by relaxing, usually too much, in order that expectations are fulfilled.

Business involves expectations. Business growth demands high expectations. Non-ownership thinking hopes for the best, conversely, a self-employed mentality expects the best. Which culture would best serve a corporation?

If it is the nature of employee-ship to have low expectations and the nature of the entrepreneurship

to set high expectations, then the task can be nothing short of evolving the former into the latter.

For an individual to evolve from employee-minded to, let us term, ownership-minded it requires overcoming previous conditioning.

A conditioning that fundamentally taught: 'do as you're told,' 'know your place' and 'don't bite off more than you can chew' as essential prerequisites for getting by. But who wants to just get by? What business will succeed in the future by just getting by?

Executives must recondition themselves to embracing the concept of taking and giving ownership. Consider, for example, the individual choosing to engage in personal development. Sooner than later, they begin to sees things differently. What happens?

Usually colleagues are very quick to put down the individual's first enthusiastic approach with the comment: 'don't mind them, they've been on a course – but don't worry they'll soon get back to normal.'

The individual's next approach then tries to initiate changes which often results in them being isolated.

A third more determined approach is to get tough. This gives their colleagues an excuse to isolate them further. Depending on their persistence, and their status level, these various approaches work to some degree, but usually only in the short-term.

Then the fourth reflective approach of 'why do I waste my time here' comes to them. From this point the individual will either fall back on the security of previously discarded habits or take the opportunity to leave. Doing so because they have reached a level of dissatisfaction with what they do. Having worked hard to develop their potential they want to continue to grow rather than be held back by small-mindedness.

They want to be able to serve and be valued for the person they have worked hard to become. It is for the same reason that many relationships fall apart, when one grows but the other party wants to maintain things just the way they are. With relationships unless there is mutual growth and respect they are doomed to either fail or drift along bound together only through habit.

From a business perspective, any transformation initiative that does raise the expectations and reward for increased responsibility in developing entrepreneurial thinking and ownership, will inevitably, be unsustainable and be viewed as just another fad with the common refrain of: 'here we go again, another change program' voiced between corridors and emails.

OK, but how do you get people to make such a dramatic change in their thinking; to move from a non-ownership employee mentality to a taking-ownership entrepreneurial mentality? After all won't they still be employees, not self-employed entrepreneurs?

Simply by changing their perceptions from a conditioned-practice into a natural-principle.

First, imagine the time when you were a child – with little to be responsible for. When you go out into the big world on your own you begin to see the world differently – yet you are still the same person.

When you make the actual commitment to live with someone you once more see things in a somewhat more responsible manner – yet you are still the same person.

When the big moment arrives and you become a father or mother you once more view the world more responsibly – you feel differently – yet you are still the same person.

Later in life when you become a grandparent you once more have a different perception – but the fact is that you are still the character you have always been – you. The only thing that has changed is the way you perceive your world.

It is not about being employed or self-employed; it is about responsibly doing neither more nor less than you should do. A company does not employ a person for any other reason than the added value that such a person will bring to a business.

If you order a pizza and the delivery boy turns up without it but wants paying anyway because he has made the trip, what would you think? As far as you are concerned he represents the pizza business you called – he is the company; he is responsible. You had an expectation and would request, even demand that he returns to his shop to get your order.

Being an employee or employer, owner or entrepreneur is not the issue. It is about knowing that you are responsible for whatever remuneration comes to you. It is about having a self-employed mentality; knowing that, as far as your own clients and customers perceive, you are the company.

If you do not fulfil such expectations then you are not being true to yourself. A company is not a living entity, it is a legal document – it is individuals that make it live and breathe. Realising that you are *already* self-employed in fulfilling expectations is the massive paradigm shift required.

In doing so you see the world differently, you take ownership because it is in line with your own expectations. You know that irrespective of whether another pays you or not, you are responsible for doing what is expected anyway – yet you are still the same person.

All that has changed is the perception that you no longer think as a hired hand, but with a self-employed mentality – like an entrepreneur.

Such a shift in thinking changes your whole outlook on what you do. It increases your energy, passion and belief in yourself. Admittedly this is a concept that is not easy to grasp.

An immediate reaction is that your conditioned thinking will utterly reject it. A secondary one is that even if you go along with it the company you currently work with (not for) will either view you as thinking above your station or take advantage of you and expect even longer hours for no extra remuneration.

The point is that having a self-employed mentality means you have a decisive choice. If you perceive that you are being taken for granted, not receiving appropriate remuneration even though you are exceeding all expectations, then you can do something about it. 'Ah, that's easy for you to say, but what about my security,' you ask. 'I can't just go rocking the boat by demanding what I want – I might find myself redundant.'

If that is the case, do you really want to work with a company that does not value a self-employed mentality, someone willing to take ownership for what they do and passionately drive it?

As for security, there is none, only opportunity. A person can work for a whole life time with only a few words between security and insecurity: 'You're fired' or 'you're redundant' or 'I'm sorry'.

Civilisations don't have futures. Countries don't have futures. Companies don't have futures. It is the people that form the companies, the countries and the civilisations that have futures. Civilisations can grow, plateau and fall off. Civilisations can last a thousand years and still fall off, companies can last a hundred years and still fall.

It is only you and you as an individual that has a future and whatever future that is will be entirely up to you. The only security is in the soul of the individual, and that security is found in the belief in yourself whenever you meet adversity that knocks you back. It is the security in your passion to create purpose in your life. It is having the security to leave your mark.

It may be that irrespective of holding a self-employed mentality you do not feel inclined to do any more because you do not feel the passion that you believe you should. In which case the words of D. H. Lawrence are appropriate: *There is no point in work unless it absorbs you, like an absorbing game. If it doesn't absorb you, if it is never any fun, don't do it.*

Y Not *question your thinking.*
Would your business improve if everyone took ownership for what they do?

Y Not *question your perception.*
Does your company treat employees differently to entrepreneurial owners?

Y Not *question expectations.*
Does your company have high or low expectations of its people?

Y Not *question your responsibility.*
Each time you have reached certain points in your life have you viewed things in a different light?

S.O.M. up v S.W.O.T down

At school history was my strongpoint and mathematics a weak one. It was decided that I should concentrate on math at the expense of history. The result was that I became mediocre at both. This thinking was in line with the school's policy to develop 'good all-rounders.'

Perhaps because we are taught at school how to get *by* rather than how to get *on* we look to enrol on how to get ahead quickly courses. In turn we are attracted to the easy and fast way of getting where we want to go rather than the hard and necessary way to achieve them.

All of us are mediocre at many things, good at some, excel at fewer and have the ability to become world-class at something. Strengths and weaknesses are not opposites and, similar to success and failure or health and illness, each follows a particular pattern.

For every one of our strengths we have many weaknesses. Where experiencing failure may be the stumbling block on the natural path to success, seeking improved strength through correcting or eliminating weakness is very much the wrong path. Yet such thinking is consistently applied throughout schools and business.

Mankind seems obsessed with correcting what's wrong, rather than improving what's right. Companies' systems seem almost rigged to catch people's weaknesses while managers spend more time working with poor performers than achievers.

Such thinking creates average and is certainly not aligned to the principles which ensure excellence. It is based on the belief that if you can identify all the weaknesses in an individual, team or company, you can then dissolve them by developing them into strengths.

Such thinking also believes that existing strengths will take care of themselves so that in the end we have people who are strong in all areas we require them to be. If someone is a natural in history, then the areas for greatest potential and improvement will be in history. But if they are weak in another subject the emphasis is put on the weak one.

When asked by an insurance company, desiring to reduce attrition, to investigate why people were leaving, my suggestion of finding out first why people stayed and then doing more of it was initially rejected. Such a common sense alternative was finally accepted with the results that more than satisfied the brief.

In accordance with the established thinking that dominates business everyday, managers spend time reviewing others. To control people you monitor their efficiency and effectiveness. The measurement for these elements is the appraisal mechanisms, but as the thinking behind them is wrong they are inefficient and ineffective.

When a company starts out it is able to concentrate on its strengths; once it is established its focus of attention is on correcting its weaknesses. When a child is very young parents are delighted about what their offspring can do; as the child gets older the parents are concerned at what he or she cannot do.

Starting school, both parents and teachers focus on discussing what a child is good at. Later, both focus on the lowest marks in a report. Such thinking seeks to root out weaknesses in ourselves and others. In considering your own habits for example, you will recall your bad ones more quickly than your good ones. Consider your strengths and weaknesses. Which come to mind first?

With our thinking rooted in improving what's wrong, the majority of our energy is spent in that area. Every day we have a certain amount of energy: physical, emotional, mental and psychic, in ascending order of importance, our psychic energy being the most valuable.

When attention is directed to what we can't do, rather than to what we can do, we unwittingly drain ourselves of our psychic energy. Chastising ourselves mentally for being bad at something, for example, will cause us to feel mentally perplexed, emotionally frustrated and physically tired.

Conversely, praising ourselves for excelling at something will cause us to be mentally stimulated, emotionally euphoric and physically energetic. This situation is rare, however, because our belief is that if you point out weaknesses and fix them, then everything will be all right. Nothing could be further from the truth, even though your rationale may shout at you: 'But you have to know what is wrong, how else can you learn to excel?'

Trying to succeed in an area where you are weak will cause you to develop low self-esteem, a poor self-image and a limited self-ideal. These are the elements that make up your self-concept, the most important command centre you have in your life. Is it any wonder that self-acceptance is lost, when we have been trained to focus our attention on what we must do to correct ourselves, rather than what we can do to excel?

Learning to recognise our strengths and developing the courage to channel our energy into developing them, will transform us into the excellent human beings we were born to be.

Those who learn how to successfully channel their energy will be the leaders and achievers in their specific fields. Those who don't will continue to feel the inner frustration associated with being unfulfilled.

Imagine a plain wall as a metaphor for a well run, successful business. Now imagine that there is a tiny mark somewhere on it. Where do you focus your attention? It travels to the mark. The established thinking of 'let's fix what's wrong' has become so obsessive that we can spot a flaw in seconds, simply because that is what we are looking out for.

Whenever someone makes a presentation, we are more attuned to its weaknesses than its strengths. Whenever we meet someone, we are more attuned to evaluating what we dislike about them, rather than what we may like. How many times are we missing the good by habitually searching for the bad?

Such thinking is always utilised when we assess others with the focus of attention being easily attracted to what ought to be corrected rather than developed. Think about your colleagues, co-workers, families and friends. What is it about them that draw your attention first.

Take the SWOT analysis regularly applied in business. Strengths, Weaknesses, Opportunities and Threats are reviewed and considered. Without exception Weaknesses take precedence over the Strengths. Every report highlights more of the former than the latter in the sincere, albeit misguided belief that what is wrong must be brought to attention.

For example in researching what keeps families together emphasis is placed on resolving the weaknesses that cause break-up, rather than on developing the strengths that bind them. Amazingly, all institutional psychology is based on what makes people depressed, rather than on what makes them happy.

Strengths will not develop on their own. Nature will remove whatever is not used, regardless of the strength of the original gift. No quality can exist without being maintained by what it attracts every moment of the day.

Many are born with genius, many with a tendency to write poetry, an inclination to sing, or some other ability. Their gifts vanish, however, if they are starved of use, as do the qualities associated with that gift.

The SWOT analysis can more accurately be termed the 'Seek Weaknesses Only Test'. The manager will spend more time with the salesman over the sales he didn't close, than those he did. He will spend more time with the clerk over the errors he has made rather than discussing the ideas he may have. He will spend more time with the receptionist over procedures of recording than on developing interaction with visitors. Tests are designed to find out what people *are not* good at, rather than to discover what they *are* good at.

The only way to develop strengths and opportunities is to ignore anything else. Applying the Strengths, Opportunities and Merits analysis, SOM, will focus the attention on what is, in the end, the only element of any importance.

When you identify your strengths and focus solely on them, your weaknesses do not count. By excelling in what you are brilliant at, weaknesses become unimportant. Athletes ensure that they only train for what they are good at.

No-one likes having fault found with what they do, yet everyone has the inclination to do just that with others. The inclination exists because of the belief that, in finding fault, we are being supportive.

It is the application of the SWOT analysis that is self-defeating because of our conditioning to focus on what is wrong.

Applying the SOM analysis helps to rebalance the focus. Over the next month only consider strengths and opportunities. Do not entertain anything relating to weaknesses or threats of any nature. When appraising another, be they a child, spouse, friend or colleague ap*praise* their merits, not their faults.

The main point of this exercise is to place the emphasis of your appraisal on improving what you can do, rather than improving what you can't do.

Rather than seek to discover why one team does not communicate or perform, seek to discover why another team does, and plan to do more of it.

Rather than seek to learn why people complain, seek to discover why others do not, and follow their example.

When the pendulum of your thinking has swung back in balance, then consider weaknesses and threats, as you can now place them in their proper perspective - be aware of them so that they do not get in your way.

SOMing up rather than SWOTing down allows you to find out what you are good at and do more of it, and to find out what you are not good at so that you can stop doing it.

I am not advocating that you ignore the weaknesses and threats, but that you don't make them the main focus of your attention.

The principle makes sound sense, so start to ignore the established practice.

Don't **base customer training programs on the 1% of difficult customers, in preference to the 99% of good ones.**

Don't **let management spend more time on why revenue is down, than why it is up.**

Don't **spend more time on errors than discussing ideas.**

Don't **prioritise over customer recording procedures than on developing customer relations.**

In all of our lives there have been occasions when we have been tested to the full yet it is because of such times that we become reacquainted with our real strengths.

As the emperor philosopher Seneca said: *It is not because life is difficult that we do not dare, it is because we do not dare that life is difficult.*

Unless we dare to discover, use and apply our strengths we will forever experience a sense of mediocrity that causes us frustration and emptiness.

Moreover we will be unable to assist in discovering, using and applying the strengths of others.

It takes courage to aspire to be who we really are and develop our strengths to the full, but we serve both society and our organisations better through our aspirations than through our frustrations.

Y Not identify your strengths

1. What most absorbs you in your work?
2. What movie roles do you associate with?
3. What was your favourite subject at school?
4. What do you day dream about?
5. What sport do you most like to do?
6. Do you delegate what you are not good at?
7. During a difficult time what did you decide?
8. What is a recurring resolution for you?
9. Do you know what others expect of you?
10. Do you know your 3 greatest strengths?
11. Are you confidently applying your strengths?
12. Do they improve when you use them?
13. Are you frustrated when you can't use them?
14. Do you get good rewards because of them?
15. Do you really apply them to the full?

If we learn to notice our own hidden strengths, we could then know what to look for in others. The traditional approach assumes that top performers have the same characteristics but to different degrees. This is not the case.

Where some human resource executives may have developed strength in empathising with everyone, others, struggling to correct their weaknesses in empathic communication, refer to compliance, company policy and budgets.

Excellent teachers treat their pupils as equals who will achieve even more than they themselves have; poor teachers present information to be memorised.

People who love their work are not even aware of the clock; poor workers are more focused on what they don't have to do.

To the good coach or manager winning means doing things right, improving the individual. To the average coach or manager winning is defined as getting the better score or bottom-line figure.

When we focus on weaknesses, it takes over our evaluation and smothers our perception of strengths. We start to feel sorry, annoyed, even frustrated at another's weaknesses. We offer pity and often criticism, which can lead to resentment as an individual's weaknesses are viewed as an impediment to the team's growth.

Improvement throughout an organisation will be created more effectively with the philosophy of aligning individuals to focus solely on their areas of strength.

Remember that the practice of recognising strengths in others can only follow the principle of recognising them in ourselves first. If we understand that our attention will be drawn first to the attributes, anxieties and insecurities that we see in ourselves, we must therefore seek to put our prejudicial observation in order first, before we seek to put others where we feel they would be best suited. If not, we are in danger of assuming what is right for them.

If, for example, a manager with a scarcity mentality evaluates a hardworking and ambitious individual, he or she will assume that this person also has a scarcity mentality. Consequently, this person is kept down, however unconsciously, so as not to threaten the security of the manager's own position.

If the entrepreneurial thinking of interviewing and evaluating everyone on the basis of doing your job were adopted the results would be dramatic.

In order to grow you have to let go. In developing others you develop yourself further.

The most valuable discovery an entrepreneurial thinker can make is about their own strengths and those of others. Therefore resources must be spent based on what people are good at, and not wasted on what they are not good at – otherwise a company loses its edge.

Strengths first start in the mind. Such strengths can be drawn from childhood yearnings, and not just current abilities. Yearnings develop which are characterized by the preferred attraction of one activity over another. The feeling of wanting to do something is triggered when you watch somebody else do it and say to yourself: 'Hey, that's not bad, I wouldn't mind doing that'.

In becoming aware of yearnings, listen to your conscience to ascertain whether they are misleading. Glamour, excitement and power make many yearn for a certain position and can distract them from their real strengths. Your true strengths are an indication of what you are to do.

This natural process is simple when followed, but most of us are not motivated in this way. We can be motivated by the friendly advice of others, or even lucrative job offers which sound appealing and may be financially rewarding but take us away from what we are to do.

The end result is that if we ignore our true strengths we end up doing what others think is best for us. When this happens our work is viewed as just work and we plan breaks away from it whenever we can.

Have you ever noticed individuals who are happy because it is the end of the week; they have finished work and are now able to enjoy themselves.

When 'I have to work' becomes 'I am my work', a release does not have to be sought, it is already there.

It is not how hard you work but how you feel about your work and how much of yourself you really put into it.

Where there is an atmosphere of instability and insecurity people can feel alienated from their companies; they question why they should invest themselves wholeheartedly in their work when there is no guarantee that they will be staying.

Many reframe their thinking to view work simply as what they do between weekends. With that thinking your work isn't really you - it's just what you do in order to earn. Without commitment there is no achievement.

Commitment is not something you manufacture, you discover it. It manifests itself when what you do is what you want. It is increased by doing what you want, by doing what you enjoy - and excelling at it.

Following your strengths aligns your commitment with your purpose by utilising your potential. How much would you rate your commitment in what you do? In hours, in money or in how much you want to do it?

The process of understanding yourself and others is completely interrelated by doing what is right for you, not simply doing the right things. The whole upwardly spiralling process develops your strengths even further.

Tide Turning Dynamics

The very raison d'être for entrepreneurship is derived from opportunity. The more common perception of entrepreneurship being risk-focused is a myth. The basis of entrepreneurship requires a willingness to take ownership, so risk-taking is viewed very responsibly. Entrepreneurship is more likely to reduce risk by using or hiring a resource rather than just owning it.

Business of course involves some element of risk as indeed the very act of living does. Think of the adage: to live and not to risk, is not to be born. Entrepreneurial-thinking, however, is about being opportunity-focused. Without opportunity to capture there would be no need for entrepreneurs and without applying entrepreneurial thinking opportunity would be neither sought nor seen.

The true meaning of opportunity originates from a time long before modern harbours when a ship had to wait for the full flood tide before it could make it into port. Aware that the cargo in their hold represented the fruit of all their ventures, the whole company aboard ship would be on the look out for the full flood tide that would carry them towards success.

They knew that if they missed it they could lose their fortune to another ship competing for the same market. At the moment the turning of the tide was spotted the cry *ob porto* would be shouted. Shakespeare aptly wove the implications of winning or losing opportunity when he wrote in his play Julius Caesar:

There is a tide in the affairs of men,
Which, taken at the flood, leads on to fortune;
Omitted, all the voyages of their life
Are bound in shallows and in miseries.
On such a full sea are we now afloat;
And we must take the current when it serves,
Or lose our ventures.

Entrepreneurship involves seeking opportunity; successful entrepreneurship is capturing the value from opportunity; and entrepreneurial thinking is maximising such value. But how can we know what is a good opportunity – one that is right for us and will create both value and reward?

Larger businesses are confused when, despite their expensive market research and development, they witness smaller or new competitors create value from what would be a perfect opportunity for them.

The way a business perceives opportunity influences what they expect to see from their market research. But the main influence is that the models they rely on relate to monitoring recognised markets. They do not monitor unrecognised markets.

Established markets may earn revenue, but it is the emerging markets that will create value. And opportunities are about creating value. Points to be aware of in seeking opportunity are:

Opportunity must create and communicate value
it is not about reducing costs or sales incentives.

Opportunity is more art than science
when you add complexity to a simple concept you lose it.

Opportunity perceived difficult is overlooked
few pursue the obvious; many later admit: 'I had that idea!'

Opportunity is perceived differently
it does not happen by itself, it is always captured.

Opportunity relates to our unconscious seeking
it follows our interest and experience.

Opportunity asks why and why not?
it is not about thinking how and how not.

Because opportunity is abundant, discernment is essential. We have to know what it is we want and why we want it; as we actually unconsciously gravitate to that which is most dominant in our mind.

Opportunity, in the world of business, is *always* right in front of our faces. The crime is that for most of our time we are either too preoccupied to be aware of it, or just not interested in looking for it.

Even if we do see it then either we don't recognise it because we are uncertain about what we are looking for, or are just too busy, or lethargic, to do anything about it.

The whole point about entrepreneurship is about seeking *new* opportunity, capturing it and creating value out of it. When we select whatever it is we are looking for and proactively pursue it we discover that opportunities relating to it actually find us. The very act of being on the look out for opportunity *creates* opportunity.

An entrepreneurial thinking culture is conducive to creating and maximising opportunity to gain significant beneficial value. Those entrepreneurial corporations that become good at it are inundated with opportunity.

One global household name generated over a staggering 6 million ideas within its organisation in one year. With each member proposing an idea every week on average it is evident that its entrepreneurial culture of putting people before products, and service before structure is highly successful. The best methodology for such innovation is the 1% Solution explained in the thoughtology Volume II: *Innovative Decisions-Allowing Creativity with Action.*

With such a magnitude of ideas it is clear that there must be a successful communication, process and reward system in place. Ideas that create opportunity are of course worthless by themselves, irrespective of how good they are. Only ideas implemented and followed through have any chance of creating value.

So, unless there is a system for distilling the ideas from generation through to evaluation and on to testing, implementation and market success, having ideas will be purely academic. Specific entrepreneurially-minded units were therefore created within this particular corporation to action the chosen ideas.

Otherwise, there would be no motivation for such an idea avalanche. The corporation is actually more an innovator to bring products to market than an inventor of products to market. So not surprisingly they are very successful at serving customers. With everyone involved in a company acting as entrepreneurial ambassadors endorsing their products through their own networks and receiving ideas in feedback they have a culture of creating opportunity and enjoying it.

Such a 'fun factor' is very often spoken about as essential to organisational culture, yet in reality is hard to attain. People that are ambassadors for what they do enjoy themselves more than people that are not. When commitment is lacking, even though they may be well rewarded and recognised for what they do, people will not be motivated to be creative nor deliver up their creativity.

History has always proved that the greater the obstacle the greater the opportunity that will be forthcoming because of the obstacle.

What is important is to never stop the process of reviewing how products and services are taken to the market; to persistently cultivate innovative ways of doing things differently and seek out gaps and niches in the market that create opportunity; and to build, and actively utilise to the full, an essential network that provides the never-ending supply of valuable ideas that maintains entrepreneurial purpose.

Too often the only question asked by business is: how can we be market leader no. 1? Whereas the real question is: what opportunities have we overlooked or ignored that we could create value from? Most market opportunities actually already exist but are simply overlooked. In reviewing how we go to market we discover these opportunities. Entrepreneurial-minded companies must ask:

What business are we in?

Why are we in this business?

What exactly is our market?

How long has our market been established?

Why was our market created?

Who is ultimately our end user customer?

What is the emerging trend in our market?

Could we lose our market?

What do we market well?

How do we currently market?

Why do we market that way?

How could we market differently?

Is our market exciting?

What opportunities have we overlooked?

What will be the new market?

Are there market opportunities elsewhere?

No one person or business is limited to one chance. Every new day brings a new beginning. Throughout our lives there are new, exciting opportunities but we have to look for them. It is pointless waiting for an opportunity to present itself – this is like standing in the middle of a park, with your hands in the air, waiting for a cricket ball to drop into them.

Opportunity does not chase us,*we* have to go after *it.*

Everyday on TV and radio and in the newspapers we hear about new discoveries which testify to the talents and abilities of the 'ordinary person' in the business world. Too many, however, think that those talents exist only in others and not in themselves, yet they are also 'ordinary everyday people'.

Every 'ordinary person' is exceptional when involved in the right opportunity, an opportunity of their own creation, making or catching. All too often we miss the boat and someone else grabs the opportunity that should have been ours.

Opportunity is under the iron law of the universe within the dominion of cause and effect. If we fail to look for it we never see it. Those who believe that you have to see something before you believe it will live their lives missing one opportunity after another. With a fresh look we can start to recognise the unlimited opportunity that lies all around us. We must learn to see abundance in what most see lack. As Marcel Proust said:

The real voyage of discovery consists not in seeking new landscapes but in having new eyes.

Often opportunities are revealed in the form of a crisis and many a success story has been stimulated in this way. In China the same two characters are used for opportunity and crisis; yet in the West we associate any crisis with anxiety; not opportunity. With entrepreneurial thinking crises are viewed as a springboard to success by opening up new opportunities.

Regardless of our line of work there is always opportunity. By learning to discard conventional disbelief and instead relating to the usually unrelated we will find all that we want materially and great satisfaction in their achievement.

All of us have sufficient ability, ideas and opportunities to enrich every area of our life. Most of us never exploit our abilities; choosing not to look at the world with new eyes, seeing only the negative instead of the positive.

If you are always waiting for opportunity, making excuse after excuse, you will reach the last excuse of all – 'I'm too old now'. Until the day you die you will feel the world was against you, your genius did not receive the recognition it deserved and those who succeeded did so because of luck or influence.

No power on earth can impede your progress as surely and implacably as you can.

You have to be your own worst and most effective enemy. You move forward when you recognise that opportunities are there for you to take as part of your right.

Becoming an entrepreneurial-minded organisation is a strategic decision. Too often strategy is misunderstood as being an operational initiative worth trying and which might gain edge over the competition.

The real role of strategy is to establish an *organisational edge* and the strategy of developing entrepreneurship establishes the definitive edge that brings greater value to both customer and organisation.

Many organisations actually lack a clear strategy. Influenced more over the strengths of the competition than their own, they are more interested in imitating than strategising.

Leaders and management that want to act strategically must develop the qualities of entrepreneurship. In this way they will be able to obtain the edge that will outperform competition and deliver the cutting edge that both they and their customers are seeking.

Making the strategic decision to become entrepreneurial is a first step; but the journey itself, similar to any change in thinking, must be continuously, supported, monitored and allowed to evolve and continue. Yet it is by far the most effective strategy for ensuring both continuous personal development and professional alignment.

Entrepreneurial thinkers move their business forward strategically seeking, pursuing, creating and then maximising value out of opportunity. To do so they hone certain characteristics.

Y Not *develop these for yourself ?*

Become aware, keep alert and stay proactive.

Capture and harness the benefits of uncertainty.

Search for what the market is missing.

Passionately pursue selected opportunities.

Adapt, adopt, improve, change or redesign.

Grow the discipline to follow through.

Focus specifically yet with flexibility.

Engage the energies of their entire network.

Become enthusiastic communicators.

Accept that mistakes make progress.

Copowerment

Why are we in business?

All of us have a yearning to know that we count for something. Each of us need to feel part of a worthwhile cause, to have a sense of purpose that gives our life and what we *do* meaning.

When life lacks meaning or direction, our frustrations drive us more than our aspirations are able to motivate us.

What are organisations? They start out as legal documents. What make them live and breathe are the people who first create them. Such people are not necessarily born leaders; have had a great idea; want to empire build; or make a fortune. They are ordinary people that are motivated by a purpose.

A business operates by making measurable returns for its products or services. It operates highly successfully with purposeful and motivated individuals.

Entrepreneurial-minded individuals involve themselves in factors that they can passionately drive with abundant energy and out of box imagination. Corporate success demands seven skills from an *in*-coming executive:

***Insight* for what the future will be;**

***Intuition* for making the right decisions;**

***Initiative* for acting effectively;**

***Innovation* for creating differently;**

***Integrity* for following through correctly;**

***Individuality* for accepting ownership; and**

***Interdependence* for supporting colleagues.**

Business is the great modern arena for individuals to express their vocation and develop potential. The purpose of an organisation is to realise its potential; and the realising of its potential lies in the strength of its purpose. Though strategies may adapt with evolving market conditions, when purpose and values prevail the organisation remains a great place to work and something people are proud to be a part of.

People that have entrepreneurial inclinations within corporations, however, often desire to run their own business. Most of them don't because of concerns over job security. Yet ask any executive what they would do if money was no object and the majority confide that they would like to run their own business.

These individuals are invaluable to creating the successful business of the 21st Century: the entrepreneurial organisation. The business entrepreneur may have enjoyed success over the past century but now it is the era of the life entrepreneur: those who want command over their lives.

These entrepreneurial individuals will expect that the company they are part of will fulfil their needs and aspirations in return for fulfilling strategic corporate aspirations. Such reciprocity demands a paradigm shift in organisational and management traditional thinking.

Having evolved from a manufacturing-driven to a market-driven and then on to a customer-driven paradigm, the challenge for business must now be to move to a relationship-driven paradigm that is responsive to the needs and aspirations of both customers *and* employees equally.

Such a challenge demands that corporate structures are customised with greater flexibility towards employees and accordingly attracts, develops and retains both them and customers. By harnessing the immense experience acquired with the customer-driven paradigm, existing structures can be adapted to function this way.

In the same way that the customer-driven paradigm recognised that customer demands could not be viewed as an annoying impediment to neat organised control systems; the relationship-driven paradigm will recognise that empowerment is no longer the powerful tool for growth it was originally considered to be.

To have power from one superior source delegated to a subordinate source does not release potential; is not conducive to instilling ownership; driving passion, or thinking entrepreneurially. The evolving life entrepreneurs will no longer expect to be treated as tools but as equity-entities of the business.

Such expectations will have to be fulfilled through Copowerment: where both management and people share and exercise power for common purpose.

Where structure has traditionally been influenced by a pre-determined fixed strategy, a service oriented Copowerment structure will provide the much-needed balance between what is important for the organisation and individuals. This will achieve the much sought after, yet elusive, alignment between organisations and the individuals that form them.

Copowerment is the key to instilling the sense of ownership and entrepreneurship that future corporations must develop to grow.

Such a practical concept of alignment relies on trust, the very foundation on which relationship-driven companies are built.

Creating a corporate entrepreneurial-minded culture involves using Copowerment to build reciprocal trust and develop agility in the structure unrestricted by boundaries.

In a relationship-driven business people are not managed, they are treated as trustworthy individuals that willingly commit their time, and energy, into what they want to do and have to do. Because they understand that there are no boundaries between the two.

This structure requires both commitment and accountability from employees. Clearly, there must be shared ownership and indeed business leaders must consider such commitment as a prerequisite to starting, or investing in, a business.

Those companies that do not allow their executives to become shareholders will have to rely on the empty promises that controlled empowerment offers for motivating their people.

For Copowerment to be effective, people must develop the trust and confidence that they are working together as valuable business-owners towards success.

Confidence and trust are best established through mutual support and reciprocal mentoring of individuals while applying the principles and practices of entrepreneurial leadership *(See Passion v Pension – published by 21st Century Books).*

Trust and confidence may be honed when times are difficult, but they are best developed through the good times in the same way that a honeymoon period helps bond a new relationship of mutual commitment.

The difficulty is that most organisations get involved in addressing cultural change more because of reducing the pain rather than seeking the benefits of the pleasure derived from improved culture.

For that reason when a company makes a strategic decision to become entrepreneurial it must adapt its structure towards one that ensures continuous learning, clarification of aspirations, and consistent flexibility to change.

The responsibility for taking action lies with the leadership of the organisation and can never be delegated.

Aspiring entrepreneurial-minded leaders must engage in establishing the template of what they want, no matter how long it takes, through co-mentoring and Copowerment with each other. Change processes that fail are due to a lack of definite action by existing leadership.

Business leaders are only human though so, often unaware that change is required, resist it because they feel secure with the way things are.

Unfortunately they have the influence to make certain that their status quo remains. The first symptom is a distinct lack of innovation or poor communication because a business becomes stuck.

Entrepreneurial-thinkers strategically use Copowerment to ensure that decision-making and ownership are close to market and customer.

E = mc² a new relativity

Where **E**ntrepreneurship = **M**arkets & **C**ustomers²

Non-entrepreneurial-minded organisations *spend* huge finance budgets on marketing, without really listening.

Entrepreneurial-minded ones *invest* their time, energy and imagination in listening to, and understanding, customers. Irrespective of the size or age of a company today, future success and growth tomorrow is relative to establishing an entrepreneurial ethos with markets and customers.

The days of *'it's a numbers game'; 'next;' 'love 'em and leave em;' 'and there'll be more where they came from,'* are over. As is the marketing textbook adage: that customers know what they want, you just have to supply it. Because customers neither want to be treated like a transaction, nor do they know in advance exactly what they want.

A customer-focused ethos involves imagining what the future holds; perceiving how market trends will shift; anticipating what the demand will be; and proactively raising the awareness of customers, thereby actually creating and becoming the future.

Entrepreneurship is about creating, implementing, driving and following through an innovative idea that seeks to maximise value from opportunity.

The hard fact is, however, that with customer awareness, competition intensity and less brand loyalty the 'innovative idea that seeks to maximise value from opportunity' is increasingly hard to bring to market and more often than not fails. The software industry, for example, has experienced a failure rate as high as 90% during some periods of its history.

In addition to this, having moved from a product-selling and customer-quantity paradigm to one of customer-serving and being relationship-driven, it is now more important than ever to know: who the customer you want to serve is; what level of relationship will develop loyalty with you; why they will want to do business with your company; and how you will attract, lead and educate them to raise their expectations and perceptions as to how your product or service will beneficially serve them.

Marketing focus is leaning increasingly inward to existing customers, as opposed to outward strangers. Cultivating and growing a customer base must involve getting to know them well in order to market to them effectively but it is, of course, vital that you clarify what market you are entering and establish the customer profile that your market comprises.

A paradox of the global accessibility is that markets are splitting into more and more niches. As they do, of course, customers become even more important, and they know it. It is vital, therefore, to know the market. Most start-up entrepreneurs get to know their market because it is local to them.

For the entrepreneurial corporation this luxury is not always available so it is important that entrepreneurial business units take on a partner, or team member, that does know the 'local' market as well as researching thoroughly at street level.

This involves visiting and getting to know the people you are targeting and then evaluating and reflecting on the research you collate. Such clarification requires a shift in thinking about both customer and market.

There are specifically 15 factors that I have identified in order to distinguish the non-entrepreneurial-minded organisation of today from the entrepreneurial-minded organisation of tomorrow in marketing and customer related criteria:

Non-Entrepreneurial	**Entrepreneurial**
Marketing strategy	Customer-focused ethos
Market size	Market niche
Customer quantity	Customer perception
Meet customer needs	Anticipate customer wants
Improve service for market	Create service with customer
Generalised products	Customised convenience
Quality imitation	Desired innovation
Customer relationship	Customer partnership
Know competitors' strengths	Understand competitors' mistakes
External market data	Close customer communication
Global scope, local focus	Global identity, personal service
Market duration	Speed to market
Market leader	Niche diversity
Marketing review	Follow-up service
Research related	Feedback reflective

Richard Branson of Virgin and Jeff Bezos of Amazon both apply entrepreneurial-thinking criteria similar to the above right hand column.

Each criterion forces a different paradigm and encapsulates the competitive advantage of entrepreneurial-minded companies. Particularly important factors are speed, convenience and follow-up.

Bezos was more interested in providing a fast, convenient, repeat service than selling cheap books. If you live in a town centre and have time on your hands to enjoy a coffee while browsing a Barnes & Noble or Waterstones bookstore that's just great. But if you don't; then allocating the time to travel to the store; getting there, looking for what you want; queuing to be served if you can't find it; waiting for it to come in if you have to order it; and phoning to see if it has come in and then returning to the store can be inconvenient and time consuming.

Being recognised as a valued customer and being offered books that similar purchases have indicated may interest you fulfils customer criteria of speed, convenience and follow-up service. The customer feels a valued partner in deciding what offerings are available.

The customer may not be aware of what he or she actually wants to read next, but the follow-up service provides guidance and suggestion on a 'why not go for it' basis, rather than 'why have it' or 'do you really need it?' basis.

Branson's Virgin Atlantic, similar to other businesses that operate under the Virgin brand, diversifies into further niche markets by creating an experience rather than just a sale.

An executive taking a flight can be collected from home and taken to a hotel before and after a flight respectively, after having enjoyed various home comforts on board which will soon include hotel and restaurant facilities. The traveller is considered a valued guest, even family member and enjoys, once again, speed, convenience and follow-up service.

Y Not ask yourself:

Does your company have a customer- ethos?

Is there clarification of who your customer is?

Has your market been clearly determined?

Are you able to anticipate future niche markets?

Is your customer perceived as a partner?

Does your customer perceive your service as fast and convenience?

Do you perceive 'follow-up' as the start of a relationship?

Entrepreneurial Networking

Networks and networking have always been the foundation stones for business building and never more so than now. Living in the age of the knowledge-worker operating within excellence-driven and relationship-driven business models such stones are vital for success.

It's not *what* you know; it's not *who* you know. It's what you *do* with what you know with who you know.

The end of the Stone Age did not come about because of lack of stones. Similarly, the knowledge-worker will not disappear because of lack of knowledge. But what they have to offer will be purely academic unless there is proactive harnessing and effective utilisation of networking in order to ensure that such knowledge is practicably applied to create value.

With the abundance of databases, coupled with the practical advantages the Internet provides, gaining access to both contacts and knowledge has never been easier. When, at the speed of thought, selected and detailed knowledge can be both sent and received it is not surprising that agile entrepreneurial business initiatives are thriving.

The speed and ease of moving information assists in maintaining communication and helping to build a network of resources. But it is not sufficient to rely on technology to build a network because entrepreneurial networks are founded on relationships.

Entrepreneurs build networks, through primary and secondary social and business networking, to overcome obstacles, open doors and access resources.

Networking is a low-cost, getting-in-touch-with-the-street methodology for learning about the marketplace and gathering information and further contacts. It involves talking to people, making contacts, keeping in touch and following through when appropriate for mutual benefit.

There are two types of relationship in networking: Firm and Fair they range from close friends and family to regular acquaintances and friendly colleagues; and Contacts, which comprise all other forms of other social interaction.

Everyone knows at least 100 people, whether Firm and Fair or Contacts. So, in seeking, creating or selecting an opportunity to pursue, it makes good sense to select those people that you already know, and believe will be willing to either provide insightful information or appropriate contacts to assist your efforts. This is where established non-entrepreneurial-minded businesses do not utilise their people potential to the full.

Opportunity ideas come from three main areas: insight into emerging trends, either through market data or reflection; inspiration that leads to something new or innovative; and from talking to people.

The entrepreneurial-thinker views business interaction with others, whether accidental, unplanned, planned, long-term, short-term or fleeting as an opportunity to construct a network of resources.

Indeed, they will either have a contact for whatever is currently wanted, or, and this is important, have no concern about immediately making contact with whomsoever they learn is the right source.

An established organisation, of course, usually has a detailed database of contacts. Indeed, it is accepted that such a database is vital. Most organisations' databases, however, are utterly under-utilised and seldom kept up to date.

Entrepreneurial-thinkers, therefore, must first ensure that there is a relevant database, reviewed regularly and applied appropriately for selected initiatives.

Secondly they must encourage colleagues and teams to develop contact lists. Such a process is in the spirit of supporting service before structure.

The purpose of the contacts list is to serve as a reminder to the individual as to the contacts that they do have, but have forgotten about. Their purpose is not to be posted for the benefit of all, but they can remind the individual of the mutual benefit of having contacts.

Whenever you meet someone, irrespective of the circumstances, there is almost always 'common ground' discovered in the form of knowing the same people. The common refrain of 'It's a small world' often leads to learning about something of interest and value and forming a relationship that provides a future win:win situation for the parties involved.

Amazingly this is rarely the case because for most of the time people do not actually network, even though they may be exposed to a networking opportunity.

I am always surprised at how people at functions choose to remain in their internal groups gossiping, rather than network in external groups with people that are often experts in alternative industries with valuable ideas and opportunities to share.

Such input of diversity will always provide added value for entrepreneurial-minded individuals, as it provides knowledge of potential markets, location of alternative resources, innovations and of course opportunity-in-waiting.

Everyone has valuable contacts. For your own valuable resource Y Not take the time to write a list of 100 contacts. The very action of this exercise will stimulate your thinking into seeing an opportunity that you have previously ignored or overlooked.

The point of the exercise is that upon experiencing the results yourself you will see the enormous value of consistently and persistently building a network for creating and following through opportunity.

Groups of decentralised units whether the 4,000 in 3M or the 200 autonomous companies under the Virgin brand network with each other for resources. And remember, it is the individuals within organisations that make things happen because of their contact-knowledge.

Too many organisations have units that keep things to themselves worry that sister units will 'steal' ideas. Lack of liaison within a corporation is a major reason for it to literally miss out on opportunity. When the strength of all resources is brought together there is greater success. Once you do make contacts, maintain them. They are an entrepreneurial resource.

Teams and Units

Entrepreneurship is an activity that creates value and is most effective when applied in a team that starts a new venture motivated by identifying a stimulating market opportunity.

It is the quality of an entrepreneurial team that is the determinant success factor in highly profitable ventures. An entrepreneurial team will initially comprise the founding members of a start-up company or 'sponsored' business unit.

It is important that the team is added to with additional increasing strength and knowledge similar to the layers of an onion. It is the role of the entrepreneurial leader to blend and grow these layers into an integrated working team.

The catalyst to stimulate the right team into right action is of course the right venture. Such value creation is their reason for being.

Diverse thinking, complementary strengths, unanimity for dominant purpose are essential for the right team as are the blending of management and entrepreneurial skills.

Loyalty and trust within the team, effectiveness of group decision making, commitment to agreed objectives and understanding of customer needs and market trends.

Forming and developing the right entrepreneurial team takes time of course, particularly because individual team members need to understand their own self-awareness, the team awareness and the strategic awareness of the organisation they are part of or that is sponsoring them as a business unit.

Above all, however, an entrepreneurial team must not get bogged down with distracting issues and minutiae, as the moment it does it ceases to operate either effectively or entrepreneurially.

The venture therefore must be highly motivating and be able to fully absorb the interests of team members. One of the challenges in ensuring the success of business units is getting teams together.

It is not necessary that a team is together all the time, indeed some of the best teams may meet only periodically while doing the appropriate work required of them. But there should never be any difficulty in bringing them together when it is required. If there is, then the team and the venture realities and commitments must be revisited.

Quite simply, any sponsored business unit must come into existence because an aspiring entrepreneurial-minded leader is passionate about driving through their selected initiative.

An organisation that identifies an initiative only to delegate it to a business unit without the buy-in of the unit's personnel is already on the road to failure. This is clearly not a rule of thumb, but it is true to say that I have witnessed many initiatives fail where the only incentive has been competitor-driven rather than commitment-driven.

Traditional organisational teams where projects are delegated to impassionate personnel and are driven by traditional methods of remuneration and even performance bonus can of course be successful. But the most important part about entrepreneurial ventures is that by the very nature of them, when they are successful they are significantly more profitable than traditional ventures. That is why large established corporations must look to recreate as entrepreneurial ones.

Companies are recognising increasingly that the real value of sponsoring business units is that it is conducive to involving the entrepreneurial-minded team that is committed to pursuing initiatives.

When compiling a team for a specific venture the criteria in selecting members to work together beyond those mentioned above are:

Does the candidate have experience in the specific industry?

Have they a proven competency record for entrepreneurial initiatives?

Will they have credibility in the industry and with team colleagues?

Are they compatible with the team, unit and corporate culture?

What network or resources are they bringing to the team?

Are they motivated to be part of the team, unit and initiative drive?

Sponsoring Initiatives

When the team have unanimously committed the organisation to becoming entrepreneurial, established an agreed support strategy and taken the time to communicate the intention throughout, then the sponsoring of entrepreneurial initiatives can commence.

Most established organisations operate under centralised leadership. Decentralised separate business units therefore should be established under the direction of an appointed, yet willing, sponsor to support these initiatives.

Once a test business unit has been established entrepreneurial 'willing' champions need to be identified and selected to operate it. These entrepreneurs, as they should be termed, must have a good relationship with the sponsor in terms of Copowerment.

Their practical training will take the form of identifying and pursuing selected opportunities within understood markets and obtaining the required resources to develop, and implement, the appropriate business plan.

The idea of a business unit should be to create an environment conducive to stimulating entrepreneurial thinking.

Indeed, there is a proven correlation between such a business unit and entrepreneurial thinking. The diversified giant 3M with its 4,000 profit centres, for example, are more like a living organism than an organisation.

What is of vital importance for the ultimate success of separate units is that the sponsor, leader or manager driving the team must be an entrepreneurial-minded leader to facilitate the right environment and lead by example. Their influence, support and expertise, will ultimately prove to be instrumental in the unit's success and growth into a larger and more profitable enterprise.

The basic rule introduced by former chairman William L. McKnight of 3M, encapsulates how decentralised entrepreneurial units should ideally operate:

'As business grows, it becomes increasingly necessary to delegate responsibility and to encourage men and women to exercise their initiative. This requires considerable tolerance. Those men, and women, to whom we delegate authority and responsibility, if they are good people, are going to want to do their job in their own way. Mistakes will be made. But if a person is essentially right, the mistakes he or she makes are not as serious in the long run as the mistakes

management will make if it undertakes to tell those in authority exactly how they must do their jobs. Management that is destructively critical when mistakes are made kills initiative. And it's essential that we have many people with initiative if we are to continue to grow.'

This approach has rewarded 3M with thousands of supported initiatives. Under the principle of 'grow and divide' small units founded on innovation and entrepreneurship are encouraged to grow into larger divisions. Indeed 3M encourage its people to devote 15% of their time to independent projects that could lead to being developed under a sponsored initiative. The 'defined project expectations' coupled with 'allocating venture resources' ensures that 25% of each units' sales is actually generated from products within five years of being initiated.

Maintaining Purpose

Moving towards being an entrepreneurial-minded organisation is one thing, maintaining an entrepreneurial purpose is another.

People make up organisations and they can insidiously become comfortable, complacent or cocoon themselves from their markets and customers because they are so busy either being successful or important. Such common action makes you mistake propaganda for purpose.

The president of a global corporation told me how easy it was to start thinking that you were some kind of demi-god when, during the good times, every one of your 100,000 people was intent on telling you what a good job you were doing.

Such invulnerability vanishes when times harden and the huge TV screens you have in your office that once displayed soaring growth begin reporting the opposite. Losing sight of your purpose and believing your own propaganda inevitably leads to receiving a jolt that, as the fallen demi-god said, 'leaves your ego teetering on the edge of a self-built precipice realising that you were mortal after all.'

The new entrepreneurial-minded corporation will sustain itself more effectively than the non-entrepreneurial-minded one because it will create *and attract* a continuous source of innovation; the key ingredient for economic prosperity.

It will also retain *and recruit* the right people for the right role with entrepreneurial spirit; the key ingredient for maintaining entrepreneurial purpose and leading the challenge.

The challenges for organisations include reducing hierarchy to flatter more decisive and agile structures that are able to swiftly respond to emerging markets and anticipate customer wants. In creating mini-enterprises within such structure they will have the benefit of a strong integrated interdependent nature that shares resources as appropriate because of its network mindset.

Such a challenge may sound like swimming upstream. To continue the metaphorical example, only live salmon swim upstream and only strong ones overcome all obstacles; in doing so new life is once again created. Old salmon die but only after having spawned literally thousands of new eggs.

Established corporations will have to come to terms with the fact that they must behave differently. The reward for successfully doing so is that hundreds of profitable business units will be created from within its nucleus. These units with their entrepreneurial-behaviour and skilled management will ensure that the new, more entrepreneurial-minded, organisation is able to fulfil its purpose of realising its potential.

Entrepreneurial thinking demands acknowledging at individual, team and strategic level the importance of lifelong learning.

Established organisations that seek a quick-fix program to introduce entrepreneurial thinking, because years of bureaucratic control that have stymied innovation are seriously reducing returns, will be disappointed unless there is commitment to a never-ending education and application of entrepreneurship.

Learning and living entrepreneurial principles builds character; and once implemented the practices improve excellence. Such principles and practices must not be viewed as a 'to do' list to mark off when mastered because the entrepreneurial leadership success they deliver requires consistency and persistency.

The nature of developing entrepreneurial leadership involves trust, courage and forgiveness. Developing confidence in such vital virtues that allow people to think as business owners takes time. The daily process of such thinking, behaviour and action is the stimulus that will drive organisations to *continuously* fulfil their potential and realise the purpose for which they were founded.

PEOPLE BUY BUSINESS BOOKS, BUT ARE TOO BUSY TO READ THEM!

Feedback from 1000's of executives has proved
a demand for High Quality Diary-Style Books
which offer Dynamic Practical Ideas and
Thought-Provoking Concepts in an accessible format.
Executives taking countless short journeys by train or plane
want something entertaining yet useful; ideas that stimulate
their thinking and can be applied daily.
Six volumes make up the collection.

Volume I	**Y Not** – entrepreneurial thinking DRIVING PASSION WITH INTEGRITY	ISBN:1-904956-06-8
Volume II	**How 2** – innovative decisions ALLOWING CREATIVITY WITH ACTION	ISBN:1-904956-07-6
Volume III	**4 You** – empathic communication SIMPLIFYING COMPLEX SITUATIONS	ISBN:1-904956-08-4
Volume IV	**Who R** – building relationships FOLLOWING THROUGH WITH SERVICE	ISBN:1-904956-10-6
Volume V	**U Can** – leadership realities SUSTAINING GROWTH WITH LOYALTY	ISBN:1-904956-11-4
Volume VI	**Will B**– motivating action WINNING BUSINESS WITH REWARD	ISBN:1-904956-12-2

To order email: **service@21stcenturybooks.uk.com**

COLIN TURNER

Passion v Pension

DEVELOPING CORPORATE ENTREPRENEURSHIP

The future is not what it used to be.
So why chase a pension when
there is no guarantee of one?
Far better to chase your passion!

Learn the Principles of Entrepreneurial Leadership
Apply the Practices of Entrepreneurial Leadership
Sustain Corporate Change with 6 Core Dynamics
Transform employee-minded managers into entrepreneurial-minded leaders

'Articulates much needed practical and effective concepts essential for future business success'
Roger Leek, Group HR Director, Fujitsu Services, Europe

'Turner directs with timely advice'
Shingo Miyake, NIKKEI, Japan

'A source of inspiration – read it!'
Frank Boyd, Head of Creative Dept., BBC

To order email: **service@21stcenturybooks.uk.com**

COLIN TURNER

Swimming with Piranha makes you Hungry

INTERNATIONAL BESTSELLER

Highly Recommended
Financial Times

Brilliant!
Daily Mail

A metaphorical must read – a unique book humorously illustrated and packed with priceless advice – essential facts to enjoy life more, work less and *have more money!*

Discover powerful practical secrets to simplifying life. Know the Seven Proven Laws vital for gaining wealth.

This book is *guaranteed* to improve the quality of your life; and *increase* your disposable income!

To order email: **service@21stcenturybooks.uk.com**

COLIN TURNER

Made for Life

INTERNATIONAL BESTSELLER

One of the classic tales of wisdom *Made for life* is both profound and extraordinary.

Delving deep, yet never becoming buried, this self-psychotherapy masterpiece provides simple answers to complex questions… …those that *everyone* asks of themselves at quiet reflective times.

'A unique book and most of all it delivers a very important message. You will love it'
Uri Geller

'I doubt very much whether anyone's life will remain unchanged after reading it'
Here's Health

To order email: **service@21stcenturybooks.uk.com**

COLIN TURNER

The Teachings of Billionaire Yen Tzu

Volumes I & II

"Hooks like a thriller you can't put down! That a book can succeed in being authoritative about success, business, lifestyle and spirituality is impressive. That it's also engrossing, inspiring and upbeat makes it essential for everyone" *Time Out*

A legend tells of a famous Academy founded some 2,500 years ago by an immensely successful Patriarch, *Yen Tzu*, teaching the secrets of a paradoxical philosophy that developed self-mastery through individual inner understanding. Such a level of understanding was instrumental in *Yen Tzu* becoming Ancient China's first commercial billionaire; though such success inevitably attracted the attention of an aspiring Emperor. History records that in the year 213BCE almost all remnants of this ancient teaching were destroyed by the ruthless Qin Shi Huang, famous for the army of life-size Terracotta Warriors whose Dynasty lasted a generation, a vivid reminder that motives seeking control are always short-lived. Unwittingly, Qin destroyed the very wisdom that would have been his greatest strength as a leader. Clearly, the application of a new thinking and practice is as valid now as it was to prosperity over two millennia ago.

To order email: **service@21stcenturybooks.uk.com**

Colin Turner is the author of 15 bestsellers published in 30 languages, including the Japan no 1: *Born to Succeed;* and the executive coaching series: *The Teachings of Billionaire Yen Tzu.* Described by *Time as 'a leading authority on business, lifestyle & management'*; he advises FTSE 100 and Fortune 500 Companies and is a thought-provoking keynote speaker at conferences. He can be contacted through: service@21stcenturybooks.uk.com or visit www.colinturner.com

His books include:

Born to Succeed

The Eureka Principle

Financial Freedom

Made for Life

Swimming with Piranha makes you Hungry

The Business Pilgrim's Progress

Lead to Succeed

The Teachings of Billionaire Yen Tzu Volume I

The Teachings of Billionaire Yen Tzu Volume II

turner's thoughtology Briefcase Series Volumes I - VI

Praise for Professor Turner's work

'What Colin Turner writes is worth reading' *Business Age*

'Creates positive results' *Evening Standard*

'Crammed full of seriously good advice' *The Irish News*

'Turner preaches what he has practised' *Sunday Independent*

'The thinking person's Little Book of Calm' *Belfast Telegraph*

'Highly researched yet intuitive'
N. Holloway MD, Microsoft UK

'East meets West for success' *His Excellency, Ma Zengang*

'Colin's philosophy works' *C. Cowdray, CEO, Claridges*

'Compulsory reading'
Dr Marilyn Orcharton, Founder, Denplan

'An excellent blueprint for success' *Sir Michael Grylls*

'The philosophy for the 21st Century'
Vera Peiffer, 'Positive Thinking'

'Timeless Wisdom' *Kyodo News*